Arctic Foxes

ABDO
Publishing Company

Big
Buddy BOOKS
Arctic Animals

by Julie Murray

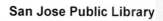

VISIT US AT
www.abdopublishing.com

Published by ABDO Publishing Company, PO Box 398166, Minneapolis, Minnesota 55439.

Copyright © 2014 by Abdo Consulting Group, Inc. International copyrights reserved in all countries. No part of this book may be reproduced in any form without written permission from the publisher. Big Buddy Books™ is a trademark and logo of ABDO Publishing Company.

Printed in the United States of America, North Mankato, Minnesota.
032013
092013

Coordinating Series Editor: Rochelle Baltzer
Editor: Marcia Zappa
Contributing Editors: Megan M. Gunderson, Sarah Tieck
Graphic Design: Maria Hosley
Cover Photograph: *Shutterstock*: visceralimage.
Interior Photographs/Illustrations: *Getty Images*: Doug Allan/Oxford Scientific (p. 17), Norbert Rosing/National Geographic (p. 9), Tom Walker/Visuals Unlimited (p. 18); *Glow Images*: Johnny Johnson (p. 27), Juniors Bildarchiv (p. 27), Wayne Lynch (pp. 9, 20, 23), John E Marriott (p. 15), Tips RM (p. 13), © Kennan Ward/ CORBIS (pp. 7, 21), ARCO/ Wittek, R. (p. 7); *iStockphoto*: ©iStockphoto.com/DmitryND (pp. 5, 11, 29), ©iStockphoto.com/twildlife (p. 13); *Photo Researchers, Inc.*: Bryan and Cherry Alexander (p. 8), Alan Carey (p. 25); *Shutterstock*: Matthew Jacques (p. 4), Wild Arctic Pictures (p. 14), Christopher Wood (p. 4).

Library of Congress Cataloging-in-Publication Data

Murray, Julie, 1969-
  Arctic foxes / Julie Murray.
      pages cm. -- (Arctic animals)
  Audience: 7-11.
  ISBN 978-1-61783-797-5
  1. Arctic fox--Juvenile literature. I. Title.
  QL737.C22M85 2014
  599.776'4--dc23
                          2012049646

Contents

Amazing Arctic Animals 4

Arctic Fox Territory 6

Welcome to the Arctic! 8

Take a Closer Look 10

Built for Cold 12

A Fox's Life 16

Mealtime 20

Baby Foxes 24

Survivors 28

Wow! I'll bet you never knew... 30

Important Words 31

Web Sites 31

Index 32

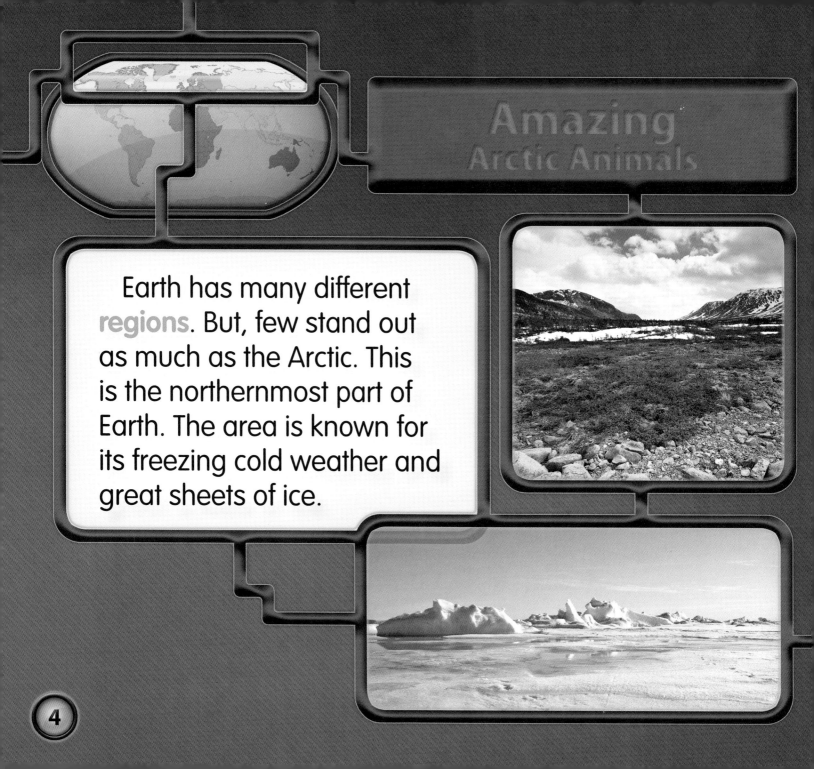

Earth has many different **regions**. But, few stand out as much as the Arctic. This is the northernmost part of Earth. The area is known for its freezing cold weather and great sheets of ice.

The Arctic fox is known for its thick, white winter fur.

The Arctic includes land from several **continents**. It also includes the Arctic Ocean and the huge sea of ice that floats on it. The Arctic is home to many interesting animals. One of these is the Arctic fox.

Arctic Fox Territory

Arctic foxes live throughout the Arctic. This includes the northern parts of North America, Europe, and Asia. Sometimes, these foxes are also found on the ice north of these **continents**.

Arctic foxes live in the tundra. This cold, flat land has very few trees. Arctic foxes often live near coasts.

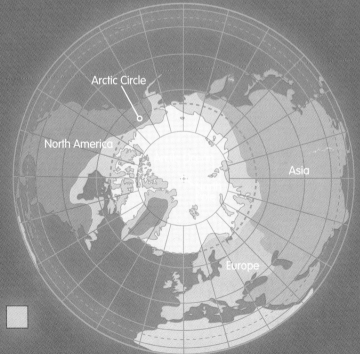

Arctic Circle

North America

Asia

Europe

Arctic Fox Territory

Most Arctic foxes have white winter fur (*left*). They live in open areas. Some have light gray or bluish winter fur (*below*). They live in areas with rocks and plants.

Welcome to the Arctic!

If you took a trip to where Arctic foxes live, you might find...

...the North Pole.

Arctic foxes have been seen by the North Pole! This spot is near the middle of the Arctic Ocean. Many historians say American explorer Robert Peary and his team were the first people to reach the North Pole. Peary traveled there by dogsled in 1909.

...polar deserts.

Much ground in the Arctic is covered in ice and snow. But, the air can be very dry. Few plants grow in these areas. They are called polar deserts.

...dark days and bright nights.

An imaginary line called the Arctic Circle rings around the northern part of Earth. Above this line, for at least one day each winter the sun never rises. But, for at least one day each summer the sun never sets. The farther north above the Arctic Circle, the more days this occurs.

SEA OF OKHOTSK

Bering Strait

EAST SIBERIAN SEA

CHUKC

LAPTEV SEA

IC OCEAN

North Pol

BA
SE

Cape

Take a Closer Look

The Arctic fox has a small body and a thick, fluffy tail. Its legs are short and thin. It has small eyes and ears and a short, pointed **snout**.

An adult Arctic fox is about 18 to 42 inches (46 to 107 cm) long. Its tail adds about 12 more inches (30 cm). An adult weighs about 6 to 20 pounds (3 to 9 kg). Females are smaller than males.

Arctic foxes have very dark eyes. Like sunglasses, they help them see even when the sun shines brightly on snow and ice.

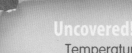
Built for Cold

Arctic foxes are well built for living in freezing cold weather. Their small ears and short **snouts** keep body heat from escaping.

Unlike other doglike animals, Arctic foxes have fur on the bottoms of their feet. And, their feet have extra blood flowing in them. This keeps them from freezing to the ice.

An Arctic fox's fur traps heat better than the fur of any other mammal.

An Arctic fox often uses its big, fluffy tail like a scarf. It wraps its tail around its face to keep out the cold.

An Arctic fox has fur that changes with the seasons. In winter, it grows long, thick fur. Most Arctic foxes have white winter coats to help them blend in with snow.

During the summer, an Arctic fox loses its winter fur. Underneath, it has a thinner coat of brown or gray fur. This helps it blend in with rocks and plants.

Blending in helps Arctic foxes sneak up on prey while hunting. It also hides them from predators such as wolverines, wolves, and eagles.

A Fox's Life

Arctic foxes are known for traveling far in search of food. They may travel in small groups. But, they generally hunt alone.

Arctic foxes form pairs for **mating**. These pairs stay together for life. During the mating season, pairs stay in certain home areas. They mark these areas with their scent. And, they make noises to keep others away.

Arctic foxes move easily over snow and ice. And, they can swim!

Uncovered!
Arctic foxes must travel very far to find food during winter. They have been known to travel up to 2,800 miles (4,500 km) in one winter!

Living in dens helps keep Arctic foxes safe from predators.

Uncovered!
Sometimes, an Arctic fox is far from its den during a snowstorm. If this happens, the fox tunnels into snow for shelter.

When Arctic foxes aren't traveling in search of food, they live in dens. They often dig their dens into hills or cliffs. Dens can be very large with many tunnels and entrances.

Some dens are used by many **generations** of an Arctic fox family. They may be used for hundreds of years!

Lemmings live in the tundra. They are the Arctic fox's most common food.

Mealtime

Arctic foxes eat almost any food they can find. This includes birds, eggs, bugs, berries, and fish. They also eat small **mammals** such as voles, squirrels, lemmings, and baby seals.

Food is hard to find during the winter. So, Arctic foxes often eat scraps of **prey** left behind by polar bears.

Arctic foxes sometimes follow polar bears for many miles to eat their leftover prey.

Arctic foxes use their strong senses of smell and hearing to find food. When a fox finds **prey** moving under the snow, it leaps into the air. When it lands, it breaks through the snow. It falls right onto the animal underneath!

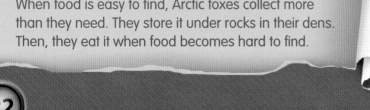

Uncovered!

When food is easy to find, Arctic foxes collect more than they need. They store it under rocks in their dens. Then, they eat it when food becomes hard to find.

An Arctic fox's ears face forward. This helps it locate prey under the snow.

Baby Foxes

Arctic foxes are **mammals**. Before a female gives birth, she returns to her den with her **mate**. A female usually has 5 to 12 babies. But when food is plentiful, she may have as many as 20!

Baby Arctic foxes are called pups. At birth, a pup weighs about two and a half ounces (71 g). That is about as heavy as a chicken egg.

Uncovered!
The Arctic fox's mating season takes place during the late winter and spring.

Arctic fox babies are also called kits, cubs, and whelps.

An Arctic fox mother stays in the den with her newborn pups. The pups drink her milk and grow. The father leaves the den to gather food.

Often, another female also lives in the den. She is usually a pup from the year before. She helps raise the new pups.

After two weeks to a month, the pups are ready to eat meat. At this time, they leave the den. The pups learn to find food and hunt by watching their parents. After about eight to ten weeks, they are ready to live on their own.

Sometimes, several related females and their newborn pups share a den.

Both mother and father Arctic foxes help raise young pups.

Survivors

Life in the Arctic isn't easy for Arctic foxes. People kill them for their fur. Food can be hard to find, especially during the winter. And, global warming has allowed the red fox to move north. It is stealing the Arctic fox's habitat and prey.

Still, Arctic foxes survive. They have many pups each year. So in most areas, their population remains steady. Arctic foxes help make the Arctic an amazing place!

Uncovered!
In addition to stealing their prey, red foxes sometimes hunt Arctic foxes!

In the wild, Arctic foxes live for three to six years.

Wow!

I'll bet you never knew...

...that an Arctic fox's tail is also called a brush. In addition to providing warmth, it helps the Arctic fox balance.

...that a group of Arctic foxes is called a skulk or a leash.

...that Arctic foxes are common farm animals. They are raised for their fur.

...that part of the Arctic fox's Latin name, *Vulpes lagopus*, means "rabbit footed." It was named this for its furry feet.

Important Words

continent one of Earth's seven main land areas.

generation a single step in the history of a family.

global warming an increase in the average temperature of Earth's surface.

habitat a place where a living thing is naturally found.

mammal a member of a group of living beings. Mammals make milk to feed their babies and usually have hair or fur on their skin.

mate to join as a couple in order to reproduce, or have babies. A mate is a partner to join with in order to reproduce.

prey an animal hunted or killed by a predator for food.

region a large part of the world that is different from other parts.

snout a part of the face, including the nose and the mouth, that sticks out. Some animals, such as foxes, have a snout.

survive to continue to live or exist.

Web Sites

To learn more about Arctic foxes, visit ABDO Publishing Company online. Web sites about Arctic foxes are featured on our Book Links page. These links are routinely monitored and updated to provide the most current information available.

www.abdopublishing.com

Index

Arctic **4, 5, 6, 9, 12, 28**

Arctic Circle **9**

Arctic Ocean **5, 8**

Asia **6**

body **10, 11, 12, 23, 30**

communication **16**

dangers **15, 18, 28**

dens **18, 19, 22, 24, 26, 27**

eating habits **20, 21, 22, 26**

Europe **6**

fur **5, 7, 12, 13, 14, 28, 30**

habitat **6, 7, 14, 19, 20, 28**

hunting **15, 16, 22, 23, 26, 28**

mammals **13, 20, 24**

mating **16, 24**

North America **6**

North Pole **8**

Peary, Robert **8**

polar bears **20, 21**

predators **15, 18, 28**

pups **24, 25, 26, 27, 28**

red foxes **28**

size **10, 24**

tail **10, 13, 30**

weather **4, 6, 9, 11, 12, 13, 14, 17, 19, 22, 23**